MW00893576

Guided Journal for Teenage Boys © 2016 by Elke Weiss

First U.S. edition 2016
Printed in the United States of America
Visit our Web site at: www.miku.media

*G*uided *J*ournal for *T*eenage *B*oys

ELKE WEISS

"Although I'm only fourteen, I know quite well why I want,...
I have my opinions, my own ideas and principles,
and although it may sound pretty mad from an adolescent,
I feel more of a person than a child, I feel quite independent
of anyone."
Anne Frank

My Journal

How to use this book:

The closer we get to being adults, the more complicated everything gets. Everyone seems to have messages for us: families, friends, teachers, and even the media tells us how to act, think, and what to want from our lives. With all that pressure it can be confusing to really know what WE want!

This book is set up as a tool of reflection on what YOU truly want. It will help you find out who you really are, what your strengths are, your dreams, your deepest and most secret wishes. Write in this book every day, or whenever you feel like it. Either go through it in order, or just open it at a random page.

Writing down the first thing that comes to mind is the unfiltered message of your inner self, so don't hesitate and start to analyze your thoughts. Sometimes it feels good to just scribble your thoughts on paper. Sometimes you want to take more time to ponder about something, so allow yourself to feel your thoughts and emotions.

If you want to doodle or draw, do it! If you need to write more, there are empty pages in the back of the book. If there is not enough space, take a sheet of paper and write, draw, or scribble more.

Get ready for a great journey into your deepest wisdom.
HAVE FUN!

Elke Weiss

What makes you happy?

What do you like about yourself?

What do others like about you?

What don't you like about yourself?

*Did something make you angry or sad today?
Jot down anything that comes to mind.*

Write down five things you are grateful for today!

- Living — having the ability to do what I want &
- My friends
- Music — (the artists I love)
- My Girlfriend
- Having the access to anything i need

What inspires you?

Who has influenced your life and how?

Did you do anything courageous today? What was it?

What makes you smile or even brings tears of joy to your eyes?

What makes you sad? What do you do to feel better?

What are some things you don't know how to deal with?
Whom can you ask for advice?

Is there something you would like to do but you are afraid of? What is it? What would happen if you just did it?

Write down five positive things about yourself.

Do friends ask you for help sometimes?
What do they think you are good at?

Write down ten things you like about your parents.

What is really important to you to feel good?

The ~~funny~~ things that i need to feel good are feeling appreciation and attention from others, and feeling productive (ish)

Finish the sentence: Sometimes I wish...

I was a little bit taller, I wish I was a baller, I wish I had a girl who looks good, I would call her. I wish I had a rabbit in a hat with a bat and a 6'4 impala.

Have you done anything today you LOVE to do? What was it?

What did you want to become when you were really young?

Who are people in your life you can trust? Make a list.

What things do you do to relax you?

To relax myself, I like to listen to music and get some time alone to think.

What energizes you?

What robs you energy?

What makes you perfect just the way you are?

What do you consider your strengths?

What are you passionate about?

Who makes you really, really angry and why? What do you to feel better?

My brother sometimes makes me really angry. Even though I love him, he recieves a lot more parental attention and love than I do (mostly because I'm adopted and it's hard for my parents to treat me exactly as their own.) I understand this and I'm fine with this, but the part that makes me angry is that he takes their love for granted and constantly is disrespectful. Despite this, they always have given him special treatment, attention, so I guess

What have you done today that you are really proud of?

What places of imagination did you go to as a child?

I'm a bit annayed at them too. I usually don't need to do anything to feel better.

What safe place of imagination could you go to in the future when you want to have a time out?

What makes you laugh? What makes your whole family laugh? What can you do to make others laugh?

What activities make you lose track of time? How did you feel?

*D*id you tell a little lie today? What was it and why?

What are you good at?

What has been the greatest challenge that you have had to overcome so far in life?

Do you feel sad sometimes? Why?

If you could get a message across to a large group of people, who is in the crowd? What would you say?

What is your biggest dream?
What is the first step you can take towards it?

What is your dream job and why?

My dream job is to become some kind of doctor. I always enjoyed helping others, and I find it an incredible feeling to do so,

What do you think you have to learn to be good in this job?

Did you smile at someone today? Who was it and why?

*W*hat motivates you?

*W*hat qualities do you possess that you are really proud of?

Did you help someone today? How did that make the person feel? How did it make you feel?

Did you do anything today to treat yourself well? What was it and how did it make you feel?

Do you think you are creative? What do you love creating?

If you could have superpowers to change the world, what would you do?

Who are the people you most admire and why?

What qualities do these people possess?

Write down three things you are grateful for today.

Write down what excites you.
Can you still do something exciting today?

What are you curious about?

Have you seen anything beautiful in nature today?

Did someone go behind your back today? How did that make you feel? What did you do? Do you think you reacted well? What would have been a better way to react?

Write about an event in your past you are really, really proud of.

Do you feel overwhelmed sometimes? When? What helps you feel better?

Can you describe the street you are living on?

Are you lonely sometimes? What makes you feel better?

What have you done in your life that you are really proud of?

Have you been embarrassed today? Why?

How do you feel today?

Did you play today? Growing up is important, but playing is important too! What playful thing can you still do on this day?

Do you sometimes have a gut feeling, but don't act on it? When was the last time you followed this feeling and what happened?

Did someone say something nice about you today? Could you accept this? Do you think they are right?

What would you like to tell your parents that you are afraid to tell them?

What makes you really, really angry and why?

Is there anything you did really well today?

What qualities do you admire in others?

When are you are depressed, what do you do?
Writing it down can help. Saying it out loud can too.

What are your strengths?

One of my strengths
is perservence, another
few could be. being open-mind
happy, and accepting.

Did you do something today because a friend wanted you to although your heart said otherwise? What was it and why did you do it? How did you feel?

Do you like yourself? Try standing in front of a mirror and tell yourself you are AWESOME! How does that make you feel?

What are you especially proud of today?

I am proud of what I have done providence so far,

What is the most difficult thing you had to go through in your life? How did you deal with it?

Are you curious about sex? Write down a list of people who you feel you can trust with these questions.

When was the last time you gave a small gift to someone who is really important to you? Can you give someone else a gift this week? What would it be?

Have you seen someone being bullied today? What did you do and why? What will you do next time?

What do you want from a friendship?
How do your current friends fit into this?

Which teacher influenced you most in your life and why?

Did you help spread a rumor today? Why? How did that make you feel? What do you feel now?

How was school today?

Do you feel you have outgrown some of your friends?
Write down why and what you need to say to them.

Do you believe in God or a higher force?
Does that belief strengthen your daily life? How?

Write down what you feel without thinking much about it. Just write what comes out ;)

Was there anything today you wished you would or wouldn't have said? What was it? Do you feel you have to say you are sorry?

Whom would you like to talk to but are afraid of. Why?

What do you want from a friendship?
How do your current friends fit into this?

Which teacher in school do you like most and why?

Which teacher in school don't you like at all and why?

What item can you use on a daily basis to remind you to breathe when things get tough? A bracelet? A rock? A symbol?

Even if your day is not a great day, what positive things happened today?

You probably know our environment is in bad shape. Do you think you can help in any way? What could you do?

Think about what you could do tomorrow that you have never done before. Write it down and remember tomorrow!

If you are angry or sad, finish the sentence 'My anger or sadness says it wants...'

Who are you jealous of and why?

Is there someone you still can help with something today?

Have you failed today? What did you learn?

We make better decisions when we are calm. What can you do to practice being calm? Write down five things.

What hobbies do you have? How you feel when doing these?

Write down some things you hope to accomplish someday!

What were some things you liked doing when you were small?

What are some things you secretly admire about yourself?

Write down three things you like about each of your friends.

*Do you like to start something new? What is it?
What baby step can you take towards it tomorrow?*

How was your day today?

If you've had any negative emotion today, write it down for five minutes and then let it be. How do you feel?

What are you thankful for today?

What do you think is AMAZING in your life?

Write down three things you would love to do more of in your life.

Do you think you are unique? In what way?

I think I am. I stand out
a lot and I am also
very outgoing to everyone.

Is there anybody whom you would love to tell what you think about them? Write down what you would say.

What are some thoughts you feel are not very helpful
and you should better let go of!

I think I should let go
of any thoughts of
weakness, as then I can
focus on improvement.

How can you organize your day better so you have
more time for yourself?

I can schedule what
I do during the day so
I do not waste precious
time.

Write down five things you like about each of your siblings.

Have you played with your pet today? Is that something you could do on a regular basis?.

What are your darkest fears?

Are you curious? Ask your grandparents to tell you a story you have never heard before!

What do you often ponder about and can't find an answer to?

What things are you happy about in life?

*What do you dream of? Dream as BIG as you like!
What could be the first step of action towards that?*

*Do you have a kind person in your life? Describe
that person!*

Write down three negative thoughts. Are they really true? What would Gandalf or Yoda say about these thoughts?

Is there anything you would like to change about yourself? What would that be?

What do you eat to be healthy?

What does love mean to you?

What does the negative voice in your head say about you? What would be the exact opposite?

What upsets you?

*W*rite down five things your parents are amazing at.

*D*o you celebrate your successes? Even the small ones? How?

Listening is important to truly understand. Whom or what have you listened to today?

Do you tend to hold problems in?
What would happen if you shared them?

Make a list of your closest friends and what you like about them.

What things do you spend your money on?

What would you love to tell your favorite teacher?

What would you love to tell the teacher you don't like that much?

*I*magine you would have a magic wand and you could be anyone you want to be. Who would you be and why?

*C*an you describe the person you want to be at the age of 30?

Are you torn about something and can't decide? Write down what each opinion has to say.

Did you have any 'Me time' today? What did you do?

Do you hold any grudges when thinking about your friends? Write down what it is, then tear the sheet out of the book and throw it away.

What do you think it means to truly love someone?

What's the best thing about your life right now?

What careers do you have in mind? Write down three choices and some positives and negatives for each choice.

What is the most fun you've had in the last year?

If you could do anything with your life, what would it be?

Made in the USA
Las Vegas, NV
06 August 2022

52827181R10056